LUCAS WAREHAN

DIGITAL FILMMAKING

The Ultimate Guide to Web Video Production for Beginners and Non-Professionals, Learn Useful Tips and Advice on How You Can Create, Film and Edit Your Videos

Descrierea CIP a Bibliotecii Naționale a României
LUCAS WAREHAN
   DIGITAL FILMMAKING. The Ultimate Guide to Web Video Production for Beginners and Non-Professionals, Learn Useful Tips and Advice on How You Can Create, Film and Edit Your Videos. – Bucharest: Editura My Ebook, 2020
   ISBN

LUCAS WAREHAN

DIGITAL FILMMAKING

The Ultimate Guide to Web Video Production for Beginners and Non-Professionals, Learn Useful Tips and Advice on How You Can Create, Film and Edit Your Videos

My Ebook Publishing House
Bucharest, 2020

TABLE OF CONTENTS

INTRODUCTION

Video marketing is one of the most powerful tools available to any internet marketer and provides an excellent way for you to set yourself apart from the millions of other people trying to 'get rich quick' online.

If you've been around the web for a while, then no doubt you'll have come across a fair number of landing pages trying to sell you e-books, 'work from home programs' or ways to lose weight. And if you're at all cynical, you will likely have thought they looked pretty much like scams – or at least bad deals.

The simple reason for this is that most of them don't look professional. They use the normal landing page design but they're written in an obvious font, with an overly salesy script and they keep saying 'Buy Now' in a big yellow button. This strategy can work for a lot of people but it also *puts off* a lot of potential buyers because it looks spammy. The average web user is becoming increasingly savvy and unfortunately for those internet marketers in their Mum's basements, that means they're harder to sell to.

So what do you do if you legitimately have something you want to sell? You need to make it look like you're *not* operating out of your Mum's bedroom. And that means working hard to create a professional looking website and professional marketing material.

This is where video marketing comes in. Video marketing impresses because it *looks* high quality. The production costs of videos are higher and if your production values *look* high, then the assumption will be that you spent a lot of money to create your advert. That in turn suggests that you are operating a professional outfit that's genuinely willing to invest time and money into a real product that you believe in.

Then there's the fact that videos are so good at grabbing attention. So good at drawing us in. So good at persuading us. If you've ever been talking to a friend with a TV in the room, you'll know how hard it is to ignore a moving image and if you've ever watched a 'Top 100 Greatest Love Songs' countdown, you'll know how hard it is not to watch to the end.

With a high quality video you can leverage all that to really sell your product and that will make a huge difference in making you stand out *and* in making your product seem like a great deal.

And here's the great part: you actually don't need a lot of money to make great looking videos for the web. And you don't need to be Stephen Spielberg either. You just need to know a few tricks of the trade so that you can approach the process logically and smartly... And precisely that's what this book will teach you.

What You Can Use Video Production For

So what does one use video production for?

One option is to create an out-and-out video advert which you can use to explain your product or service and make it sound desirable. Form here, you can then place that video on your homepage so that anyone that visits your website will get a good introduction to your business and what you do, or you can use it through a number of other channels. Good options include Facebook, where you can use a 'Page Post Video advert' to reach a large audience targeted for your specific audience.

Another option is upload your video to YouTube or Vimeo where you can actually get a lot of viewers if you think about getting the title, description and keywords right. Here it often makes more sense to take a less direct approach – instead of making your video an advert for example, you can make it a 'vlog' where you talk about something people will find interesting and then promote your video right at the end.

Selling a fitness e-book? Then you can make a professional looking video on how to build strong pecs, upload it to YouTube, Vimeo or Vine and then make sure there's a call to action at the end.

Video marketing can also be a useful addition to a range of other marketing methods and strategies. One particularly good example of this is Kickstarter. Kickstarter is a website where entrepreneurs, start-ups and small businesses try to raise funds for projects. Instead of trying to get

$2,000,000 from a single investor who wants to profit, they instead try to get $10 from 200,000 potential fans who just want to see the project become a reality. Kickstarter was responsible for the huge successes of the Oculus Rift, the Pebble Watch and even countless games and films. But to succeed on there, you *absolutely* need a fantastic video.

Finally, video production can be a product in itself. Either you can offer video marketing services for other people on the web (and actually earn a lot of money in the process as this isn't a very competitive area) or you can provide attractive videos as part of your product. 'E-Courses' for instance sell very well online and are much more appealing with a video element.

WHAT YOU WILL NEED

So that's why you should learn at least basic video production. This is potentially highly lucrative and it can help you to be more successful in *all* your web related activities. But how do you go about it?

To begin with, you are going to need some basic tools...

Hardware

Hardware-wise, the most obvious thing you'll need is a high quality camera. This should be something with a wide angle lens, which a good framerate and with a high definition. Of course you can look into recording in 4K if you're really serious about making something high quality, but for most people a cheaper HD camera will be fine as long as it's 1080p. These smaller files also make life a little easier when it comes to uploading and storing them.

Another piece of equipment you will need for making high quality videos is a microphone. If you've ever tried recording without one on a camera that's less than professional quality, you'll know that it can sound echoey and muffled and that there's often traffic and other noise in the background. That's not exactly professional! To avoid this then, invest in a mic that you can wear and that will feed directly into the camera. This is less crucial but will make a big difference.

More option is to consider getting a second camera. Having two cameras is very useful if you want to do some fancy editing, for instance you can have more than one camera on your subject at a time as they talk and this will help then let you cut to different angles. This is a technique you'll notice if you watch any other professional YouTube videos, or if you ever watch the news.

There are also a number of other optional extras. For instance, you may be interested in getting professional lighting equipment which will also upgrade your videos. Likewise, you might want to get some professional white backdrops. These things are expensive though, they take up a lot of space and there are ways of getting around them with cheaper alternatives – all of which we'll be looking at.

Of course you will also need somewhere that you can edit all this video. That means you'll need a fairly decent computer and as a minimum this should probably be an i5 processor with 4GB of RAM. The higher the quality footage though, the more power you'll need to manipulate it. A tripod for your cameras is also a smart move.

Video Production Without Hardware

Believe it or not, a video camera is actually an *optional* piece of equipment for professional video production and you don't actually *need* it in order to make something that will help you to sell your products or services. The reason for this is that you don't actually need to be in your own videos and nor do you need anyone else to be – instead you can simply feature a slideshow, text or a cartoon. Some of the software we will look at later on such as Easy Sketch Pro will talk you through making videos without the equipment which is a great budget option.

Software

Software wise, a good starting point is with your basic editing software. If you can afford it, then the best choice here is to use Adobe Premier. You will need to buy this as a subscription through Adobe Creative Cloud, or alternatively you can get it on its own more cheaply. Getting Creative Cloud makes sense though, as it gives you access to Adobe After Effects too, which allows you to make a lot of fancy edits on top of your basic editing.

If you don't have that kind of money, then you can alternatively use the free software that comes with most PCs called Windows Movie Maker. This lacks some of the more advanced features of something like Adobe but is suitable for very basic editing.

Specialist Software

There are also a number of other options available to you. Video Maker FX for instance is a great 'all in one' video making software that is very popular among marketers and businesses. It streamlines the process of editing videos and introduces a lot of useful tools specifically for creating adverts that will sell products or introduce services.

Another great choice is Easy Sketch Pro. Easy Sketch Pro is the software that marketers and businesses use to create those 'hand drawn whiteboard' videos. You will likely have seen these on YouTube and business sites yourself – they involve a hand moving around a whiteboard and drawing the thing that you are talking about – you simply narrate over the top.

These are eye-catching, light hearted and professional and they're a good choice when you don't want to stand in front of a camera and don't want to invest in the necessary equipment. In many ways this can also look more professional – if you can't film and edit professional quality footage then you're normally better off *not trying to*. It's better to avoid creating that kind of video altogether than it is to try and fail.

Another option is Explaindio. Explaindio is a similar piece of software that is designed to allow the integration of animations and HD video. It's perfect for creating marketing, explainer and training videos very quickly and can again save a lot of time and trouble compared with doing it all in an editor.

Explaindio also has a video converter tool that can be used to alter the format of videos as necessary and which can thus be used to ensure your video files are suitable for use on YouTube or however else you intend to use them.

PLANNING AND PRE-PRODUCTION

Before you get started creating anything, you need to know what it is you're going to create. This will then inform the process you use and which tools you're going to need.

Deciding on Your Type of Video

The first decision is what kind of video you're going to make. We've already seen that tools like Easy Sketch Pro can be used to make videos without the need for cameras, sets and lighting etc. At the same time though, this does limit you to 'whiteboard animation' videos. You might alternatively decide to make a slideshow, which will also impact greatly on the requirements and time investment.

The correct solution here is ultimately going to depend on the purpose of the video. Here are a few different examples of uses for your videos and of how that might impact on the type you decide to make…

Video for a Landing Page: Often if you head to a landing page (a page entirely designed to encourage a subscription to an e-mail or the purchase of a product), a video will play that explains the value of the product and tries to persuade you to buy. These are the sorts of videos that start with lines like: 'Hey you, ever thought that there must be an easier way to get ripped, six pack abs?'.

These videos are very simple and the focus is intended to be on the content rather than the production. In this case then, you can definitely keep things simple and use a tool, use still images and edit them together in video editing software, or even just save a PowerPoint video as an .mpg which you can do in Microsoft Office as of 2010. Then all you need to do is to narrate the video.

Videos for Businesses and Services: You might also find a video on the homepage of a company, explaining what they do so that visitors can easily understand. To make these kinds of videos, you will likely want to use one of the tools above such as Easy Sketch Pro or Explaindo. This increases the production value of what you've created over a simple slideshow but it also looks professional because it keeps you *out* of the video. For B2B services, you want to try and avoid being too 'personal' and this is a good way to achieve that. Again this type of video will likely be narrated (or will use subtitles) and you'll probably want to include some music as well.

Adverts: In other cases, you will be using your video simply as an advert. Perhaps for instance, you want to post a video ad to Facebook promoting an app. This way, you can show your app in action, you can explain what's so good about it and you can elevate your business and appear more professional at the same time.

These kinds of adverts require a little more care and will usually be filmed with a camera and edited in Premier/After Effects. You'll want a script, some music, a storyboard, a narrative and more.

Vlog: A vlog is a video you'll post to Vimeo, YouTube or Vine in order to build a following. This is a form of content marketing and can be used to establish yourself as a thought leader and to thus become an authority who can recommend products.

This kind of content gives you a lot more flexibility to think about how you want to present yourself and tends to be more personal (often vloggers will have a personal brand that includes their personality as a selling point).

If you look at 'big' vloggers on YouTube, you'll find they all approach their editing and filming very differently. ColdfusTion is a relatively new personality who uses very high production values to create artistic documentary-quality videos on technology. In his case, it's the attention to detail that goes into the editing that has helped make him a success.

Meanwhile though, you also have the likes of Elliot Hulse. Elliot is a personal trainer who gives fitness advice on YouTube and for the most part, he does it in one take in his gym and with no editing. He too is incredibly successful.

Others: There are other kinds of video too. Kickstarter videos for instance will be a little closer to an advert with some interview elements. Meanwhile, videos for e-courses might be more akin to a high quality vlog. Think about the purpose of your video and then look at how others that are successful in your niche have created that kind of content.

Storyboarding

The next step in the process is storyboarding. This means putting together the plan for your video – and if you do this at the start then it can save you a lot of trouble.

This is very useful in particular if you're making an 'advert'. Here you will likely have a narrative thread and the purpose of your filming will be to convey that 'story'. You can do this by carefully selecting your shots to best portray the emotion and what's happening. Switching angles can also help and if you watch other adverts, you can start to get a feel for the conventions.

How will you open? With a long shot of people enjoying your product? With footsteps running in the sand? With a dark screen and your logo?

Draw this up as a comic book and follow your instincts. This way, you can save time when you shoot the video. It may not be necessary though if you're just making a vlog or a slideshow.

Creating a Script

What a slideshow *does* need though is a script and this is something that you're going to use in pretty much every type of video.

This is important as while the imagery and music might capture the attention and convey the emotion – the script is what's going to inform the viewer and ultimately persuade them to buy.

The key to remember here is that most people are in a hurry when they're online and will tend to have short attention spans. The last thing they want to do is to watch a 20 minute video on a subject and YouTube statistics reveal that shorter videos perform better... ...*although* an exception to that rule may be for slideshows on landing pages. Why? These are often very 'long form' and will even skip the ability to jump forward because they want their viewers to feel committed to the product. The logic is that after listening to a video for 20 minutes, you're going to want to buy the product just so you feel you haven't wasted your time!

Still though, even these types of videos need to focus on grabbing attention quickly, drawing the viewer in and preventing them from wanting to move on. You do this by avoiding lengthy intros and by getting *straight into* the meat of the subject. You can also utilize an element of mystery and curiosity don't necessarily say how your product works just say what it can *do* for your viewers.

This distinction is important. When trying to persuade in any type of speech or text the key is to focus on what is known as the 'value proposition'. This answers the question: 'what is it that you're really selling?' Or 'how does someone benefit from using X'? To illustrate this point, we can turn to the old saying: you don't sell hats, you sell warm heads.

So if you have a book on personal finance you're selling through a video, the start of that video should focus on what it might *feel* like to be free from money stress and debt. Perhaps you might talk about the things that you would buy if you had lots of money. Maybe you'd talk about how much more confident you feel when you have money.

"And this book is the *actually very easy* way you can have that kind of wealth *within two years*. How does it work? Keep watching…

"I was just 20 when I discovered…"

You see? This kind of format grabs attention and it motivates you to keep listening. You can then either use the long approach with a long video explaining (in vague terms) how your system works, or you can quickly outline the key points of what your product does and then motivate a quick 'call to action' (AKA sale).

If your video isn't about short-term sales though, then you might leave out the call to action and instead just reinforce your brand. Or, if you are selling a B2B product, you might be less emotive and simply talk about the hard facts. You'll find that the correct approach does vary somewhat depending on your goals.

Finally, for all but B2B business descriptions, you should consider using a narrative. For an advert that can be a movie-like narrative that is told through images and dialogue. For a slideshow or animation, you might opt to have a first person narrative that tells the story of how you discovered your 'secret recipe' or 'business model'. Naturally, we are inclined to listen to stories and this is a great way to really sell the emotion of what you're saying. They engage quickly and make it hard to stop listening.

The following tips can also help you to ensure your script works well:

- Appeal to facts, figures and people in positions of authority. This will help you to better encourage your audience to believe your points.

- Include 'social proof' if you can, in the form of customer reviews and quotes

- Ask rhetorical questions – these improve engagement because they encourage us to reflect on what we're hearing

- You also want to be more conversation than you would be when writing. Of course the tone still needs to be appropriate for your particular business and niche – but even then a B2B script is going to sound more 'chatty' when read than it would do when written. This is also another benefit of using rhetorical questions.

FILMING AND PRODUCTION

How to Read Professionally From a Script

Now you have your script, the next step is to read from it. This should be done in such a way that it sounds conversational (not robotic) but at the same time it should also be professional without stutters or 'filler' words (um, ah, err).

Print out your script onto some paper and try reading it slowly. Take a pause after each sentence and try to 'read ahead' so that you don't get any surprises. Another good advantage of reading more slowly and with pauses, is that it allows you to more easily edit the sound later on. Just restart the sentence if you hiccup and you can always remove the problems in post-production.

Some Tips for Using a Camera

Editing will also come to your rescue when it comes to filming – but it does help to have good raw footage to start with.

One tip then is to film longer than you think you need to. Have a pause at the start of the video and at the end of each take and this will make it much easier for you to edit it together later. Another tip is to use multiple angles on each shot if you can, so that you have more options again in editing.

For static shots – such as shots of people talking – you should always have the camera on a tripod and should keep it level. For shots with more movement, having the camera move as well can help to make your footage more dynamic and engaging. Think panning, sweeping and following.

There are lots of ways you can do this without necessarily needing a professional steady cam – for instance you can attach it to a swivel chair from an office (if you have a flat floor). Sometimes a handheld shot can work too – but think about what you're *saying* with that shot (following people running with a handheld shot makes sense for instance). Don't have imperfections that are there just because you didn't think about them or it was easier that way. **Note:** YouTube also gives you the option to apply image stabilization which can avoid some shaking that is unintentional.

Another consideration is lighting. The idea here is to make people look their best and to do this you can try using Rembrandt lighting (which lights just a third of the face). You can do this with lights, or by sitting by the window.

In more dynamic shots, the lighting should be used to create drama (avoid having your camera point into the light most of the time) while when using a white backdrop, the aim will be to remove shadows.

Think as well about the composition of your shot. Do you want things in the foreground? How are you going to create a sense of depth? Will you blur out the background with macro?

Creating Your Set

Also very important, is to think about your set. If you're creating an advert or a vlog video, then this will have a big impact on how professional the production seems.

As mentioned, one option is to use a white backdrop. You can either buy a canvas for this purpose, or you can use a tightly pinned bedsheet that has been thoroughly ironed. Using a white backdrop of either kind, or a green screen, will make it easier for you to add effects subsequently too and makes a very professional look. If you struggle to get the right effect with a bedsheet, then another cheaper alternative is to find a green screen or white room that you can rent – have a look on Google and you'll probably find local ones.

Otherwise, good places to use include crowded spaces (with blur to avoid distracting the viewer) such as beaches, parks and shopping centers.

Another option is to use a place of work – which works well for business videos and start-ups on Kickstarter. Alternatively you can create your own 'set' at home – clear some space, rig up a flatscreen TV or monitor to show your logo and sit behind a table with a cloth over it. You might also add a couple of interesting items to your backgrounds.

EDITING

How to Use Editing Software

Once you have all your footage, you'll then import this into your editing software. From there, you can drag and drop each file into your timeline, where you'll be able to set the start and end points and choose transitions.

Transitions are the animations that occur between each clip. These tend to be used when you're changing from one scene to another – not when you're switching angles on the same shot. A good transition can add more interest to your video and more movement but do try to avoid a situation where they're distracting from the content itself. This is a situation where often 'less is more'.

Another time to use a transition is if you are moving from one video to another one that's very similar. If the camera angle is similar between two shots, then a cut can look jarring as it will look like you have skipped several frames. This can sometimes be used stylistically – especially for vlogs – and is what you call a 'jump cut' (it's great for comic effect).

Otherwise, use a transition to show that what they're seeing is definitely an edit or switch to another angle.

Another tip for editing, is to try and keep your shots shorter – especially for action shots. If you pause too long between angles it will again draw attention to the fact that it has been edited. On the other hand, jumping straight out of one movement to another is a great way to keep the energy high in the video.

Openers, Music, Logos, Titles and Lower Thirds

To further make your videos look professional, there are a few extra things you can add.

One example is an opener. A video opener is a short 'intro' to your video which makes sense if you're creating a series of videos (such as a course or a vlog) rather than a single standalone video. Openers often appear at the very beginning of a video, or after a brief spoken introduction – take a look at some other videos on YouTube to get an idea.

If you don't have the skills to make your own video openers, you can hire someone to handle it for you either through a site like UpWork or Elance, or even on Fiverr. Bear in mind though that it doesn't have to be extravagant – a static splash screen or short montage of your best clips can work wonders.

Another thing that can elevate your video is to add your logo to the bottom or top of the video. This branding can help to tie your video more closely to your brand and it prevents people from stealing your footage. Creating a logo with transparencies will make it more seamless in your video but make sure it works on multiple backgrounds as the color will change a lot in your video.

'Lower thirds' are a convention of video that involve adding titles to the 'safe' section of your video (the lower portion). You can normal add things like names of people you're interviewing here and it won't cover up faces or other key elements. Add some animation to your lower thirds (applying 'ease in' and 'ease out' as well for a more organic feeling movement) and keep their style consistent in order to ensure that your visual style doesn't jump around. You also want to think carefully about your fonts – and you can find a ton of free ones to use at FontSquirrel.com. Of course you can also use titles in other ways – such as between cuts.

Music is also very useful for getting more emotion out of your videos and will help to add an even more professional sheen. You can make your own music using tools like Fruity Loops (premium music creation software) or even Music Maker Jam (free for Windows 8). If you know a band, that's another option, or you can look for stock music or pay someone on Fiverr/Elance.

Do be cautious here though – if your music is too loud it can make the voiceover hard to make out and this can really undermine your message and frustrate viewers! Again: less is more. (If you're unsure, try asking a few friends or co-workers for their opinion).

Closing notes

As with many of these things, the best way to get good at video creation is to get stuck in and to start trying. Don't expect your first video to be a masterpiece – try doing something a little less ambitious to begin with, such as using Easy Sketch Pro. After that, you can then try learning from your experience and moving on to more taxing projects. You should find it's surprisingly fun and once you have built up confidence in the skill, you'll be able to drive sales and build recognition like never before!

Printed by Libri Plureos GmbH in Hamburg, Germany